28 Days to a New YOU!

—

SHELLY WILSON

28 Days to a New YOU!
By Shelly Wilson
Copyright © 2013 Shelly R. Wilson
www.shellyrwilson.com
Bluebird House Publications

All rights reserved. No part of this publication may be reproduced, distributed, or transmitted in any form or by any means, including photocopying, recording, or electronic or mechanical methods, without prior written permission of the publisher, except in the case of brief quotations embodied in critical reviews and certain other noncommercial uses permitted by copyright law.

Disclaimer: The information in this book does not substitute for medical care. Do not discontinue use of medication, or disregard the advice or your medical professional. This information is a supplement to any current health care treatment, and is not intended to diagnose or cure. Always consult your doctor. The author and publisher of this book are not responsible for the actions of the reader.

Cover design and formatting
by Lloyd Matthew Thompson
www.StarfieldPress.com

Shelly R. Wilson
Intuitive Medium ~ Reiki Master ~ Spiritual Teacher
36511 S 4450 Rd
Vinita, OK 74301
(918) 782-4778
www.shellyrwilson.com
shelly@shellyrwilson.com

28 Days to a New YOU!

~ CONTENTS ~

Lisa,

thank you so much
for being you!
I value your presence
in my life.
I appreciate your
support and
encouragement.
with love,
Shelly

*This book is dedicated to all who are embarking
or continuing on their own spiritual journey.*

I am grateful for my family and friends and ALL of the
experiences I have had.
I acknowledge your presence in my life,
I value our relationship,
I appreciate your support and
I love you tremendously. I am so thankful for YOU!

~ Foreword ~

It is a great honor for me to be one of the first to read this important book. Honestly, I couldn't resist the title: *28 Days to a New YOU* called to me on a soul level; and I think this is because I am always short on time, and the thought of making such significant progress in less than a month was very attractive to me.

As someone who has channeled Spirit for nearly three decades, I know that receiving guidance is always easier than incorporating that guidance into one's daily life. Why? Because tuning in to advice and wisdom is only the first step. The true challenge of being human is mustering the courage to examine our lives, recognize our life scripts, spot our windows of opportunity, and put that wonderful advice and wisdom to work for us. And doing that...well, that takes strength, and it takes work. This kind of work is really an investment; and it's one that pays big dividends as we grow spiritually, as we recognize our true power, and especially as we move ourselves forward to become who we are meant to be on this physical plane of existence and fulfill our true purpose.

Synchronicity is an interesting thing, full of positive energy and intent. By picking up this book, you have found yourself at the gateway to spiritual advancement, and you will no doubt find, as I already have, that these pages are chock full of important guidance, advice and wisdom. Author Shelly Wilson has also provided us with exercises that are deliberately thought-provoking and challenging; exercises that absolutely open our minds, our hearts, and our souls. By meeting the challenges; and yes, by doing the homework the author has given us, we will enjoy the benefits that come with investing time and thought in ourselves: We will take control of our lives, our power, expedite our spiritual growth, discover who we are and what makes us tick, and create a new and better version of ourselves.

If truly understanding yourself, loving yourself, and living an authentic life are on your to-do list, then you are synchronistically in exactly the right place: start investing in yourself right now by turning to page one of this enlightening and insightful book.

Sherri Cortland, ND
Spiritual Growth Expeditor and Author of
Windows of Opportunity, *Raising our Vibrations for the New Age*, and *Spiritual Toolbox*

www.SherriCortland.com

I loved reading Shelly's book, *28 Days to a New YOU*, and I know you will too. Authentic, compassionate, and steady guidance greets you on every page and you feel like you're having a cup of tea (or in my case, a delicious latte) with your best friend. Each day, you receive the gift of transformational inspiration, delivered right to your "door" in the style that I am a huge fan of - keep it simple, easy, and powerful. Shelly's book is chock full of deep wisdom and powerful exercises to assist you to shift your vibration. You are encouraged to use what resonates with you by tuning into your guidance. Get ready to... discover who you really are, fall in love with your true self, learn to trust yourself, and above all know that all is well.

Jill Lebeau
Co-Author of *Feng Shui Your Mind ~ Four Easy Steps to Rapidly Transform Your Life!*

www.FengShuiYourMind.com

When I first heard the title *28 Days to a New YOU*, I wasn't sure what to expect, but knowing Shelly Wilson personally allowed no doubt in my mind that it would be something amazing.

When she offered me an advanced copy of the book, I quickly discovered I was very wrong— *28 Days to a New YOU* is **astounding**!

In all things, you must begin with your own self, first and foremost. In these pages, Shelly very simply and logically lays the groundwork for those serious about taking their empowerment into their own hands. She suggests dedicating as little as four weeks to sitting with yourself— only a few moments a day to connect with your Inner Self. She guides you to truly listen what your Self is telling you. The included "Questions To Consider" are especially insightful, sending you down many paths of contemplating and introspecting, at the perfect moment each and every time.

There is a hidden meaning in the word "New" that I've found many misunderstand. New certainly *is* the freshness and sparkling shiny-ness that it first brings to mind, but what many overlook is that New is also *change*.

Think of, "Out with the old, in with the new." There are many things in this life that require trading in the old when you acquire the new. You have no room for both things, or simply cannot afford the upkeep on both things at once. And so it is with your own life—

you cannot afford to keep the old *and* the new. In fact, it is quite impossible to do so.

Change is what is called for in order to grow, and change means letting go of something else, such as old ways of thinking and acting. This takes effort and work.

So you want a new you? You would not be holding this book if some level of your being did not! And I can say from my work side by side with Shelly, that you have come to the right place, and you are in a safe space here. A sacred space.

Open your Heart. Examine your Soul. Choose who *you* wish to be.

No one but you can do this for you.

Lloyd Matthew Thompson
Author of *The Galaxy Healer's Guide*, and
The Energy Anthology chakra series.

www.GalaxyEnergy.org
www.StarfieldPress.com

28 *Days to a New YOU* is an informative, practical, and fun read that is your personal guide to transforming every aspect of your life. This book is an absolute must read for those who are looking to empower themselves to change their reality.

Larry Flaxman
Author of *This Book is From the Future: A Journey Through Portals, Relativity, Worm Holes, and Other Adventures in Time Travel*;
The Trinity Secret: The Power of Three and the Code of Creation;
The Déjà vu Enigma: A Journey Through the Anomalies of Mind, Memory and Time;
11:11 - The Time Prompt Phenomenon: The Meaning Behind Mysterious Signs, Sequences and Synchronicities; and
The Resonance Key: Exploring the Links Between Vibration, Consciousness and the Zero Point Grid

www.LarryFlaxman.com

28 Days to a New YOU!

—

SHELLY WILSON

I wish to ask you…

Are you simply existing or actually living your life to
the fullest degree possible?

Are you ready to let go of the past, live in the present,
and look to the future?

Are you ready to live an authentic life and be the best
you can be?

Are you ready to learn to love yourself?

One of the most tragic things I know about human nature is that all of us tend to put off living. We are all dreaming of some magical rose garden over the horizon - instead of enjoying the roses that are blooming outside our windows today.
*~ **Dale Carnegie***

~ Introduction ~

As an Intuitive Medium, Reiki Master and Spiritual Teacher, my personal mission is to assist others on their own journey into consciousness while encouraging them to live an authentic life through awareness and empowerment. Coming from a place of respect, truth, integrity and love, I honor your free will and recognize that you are co-creating your reality with the Universe. My intention is to bring understanding, help you to heal from the past and realize your full potential. I invite you to begin your life in a new way and tap into your inner power as you explore who you really are. Refrain from simply existing and elect to live your life fully without regret. It is time to let go of the past, live in the present and look to the future for it is this attitude that will transform you.

The world we have created is a product of our thinking;
it cannot be changed without changing our thinking.
~ Albert Einstein

I have chosen to write this book to assist you in your transformation. The topics covered in this book were originally visited in my DailyOM course, *Stop Existing and Start Living!* Having written the course over a year ago, my guides recently nudged me to revisit what I had written and revise and update the material. In addition, I realized that a course has the energy of studying and coursework, which may leave many people with the feeling of obligation so they choose not to participate. The energy of a book in my perception is completely different; it is simply meant to be read and absorbed without doing any "work" per se. With that said, you may be guided to read this short book in its entirety or read it one day at a time.

There is a belief that it takes 21 days to change a habit. This is an average assessment as some individuals may take longer to modify what they wish to change; whereas some people can do so very quickly. Personally, I feel that the time constraints should be eliminated altogether, and one should focus primarily on being present. I have picked the number 28 simply because there are 7 days in a week and 4 weeks in a month, which means this book offers 28 days of guidance with each day focusing on a specific topic. I believe that transformation is continual and never-ending. Your intention for choosing change is significant.

Why do you want to change?
Who do you want to become?

There are a couple of ideas that I would like to suggest to increase your chances of having the outcome you desire. The first and foremost is to be kind to yourself. Allow yourself the opportunity to take baby steps. As you shift your perception, you will change your experiences, including those in the past, the ones you are presently experiencing and those that have yet to happen. This transformation involves altering your mindset and attitude as well as your thoughts, words and actions. I recommend identifying an accountability partner or two. This friend or family member should be someone who is willing to listen to you and also tell you the truth when you ask for advice (and even when you don't directly ask). They should be someone that you trust and can count on to be there for you. They are your support and will help motivate you.

Meditate

In addition, I believe that meditation is important. Take time each day to connect with YOU— your inner self— through meditation. Whether you enjoy sitting silently in reflection, listening to a guided meditation, spending time outdoors in nature or going for a walking awareness meditation; meditation will enhance your life tremendously. For some individuals, reading is a form of meditation. The intent of meditation is to just BE and listen. Allowing yourself to listen to the guidance you are receiving and to be present in the moment will assist you in your transformation.

Take a moment to breathe in deeply and exhale anyone and anything that no longer serves you. Be mindful of your inhalations and your exhalations. Two to three times a day for 2-3 minutes, clear your mind and open your heart. Doing so will assist you during this transitory period.

Perhaps, you may even be guided, just as I am, to pause from what you are doing, close your eyes, sit silently for a few minutes to connect, and then resume the activity. Throughout the day and even now as I am writing, I will do exactly that. I stop when I am guided to. Although it may be just for a few minutes, those minutes have an extremely powerful effect. Not only do I feel refreshed and energized, but my concentration is typically enhanced, and I am able to accomplish more in less time.

Journal

Journaling daily is recommended as it will assist you in recognizing who you were, who you are and who you are becoming. Write down your thoughts, feelings and emotions as you are guided to do so throughout the day. Pay attention to bodily sensations as well. Read back through what you have written whenever you are guided to.

Keep in mind that there is no right way or wrong way to journal— only *your* way. You may opt to keep a handwritten notebook or maintain a document on your computer or even both as I do. Do not constrain your expression by feeling obligated to write for a specific amount of time. Simply allow the words to flow. For many individuals, their blog is their journal. I can attest that journaling assisted me greatly with my awakening and opening up to Spirit. Plus, it really helps me to remember my dreams.

Daily Message to Uplift

For each day, I am offering a message to uplift your Spirit using Doreen Virtue's *Healing with the Angels* oracle cards as a Divination tool to assist me in the process. The cards I pulled for each day are displayed in bold. The accompanying message is my insightful interpretation. I encourage you to go within to interpret the meaning of the messages for you specifically.

Since we each have freewill, practicing discernment and acknowledging what feels right to you is essential. If any of the information I have provided does not resonate with you, please practice discernment and choose not to accept it for yourself. In other words, accept what resonates and discard the rest. Do not feel like it has to be all or nothing.

Not everything that is faced can be changed,
but nothing can be changed until it is faced.
~ James Baldwin

This is your life!

This is your transformation!

Become an active participant in becoming a new YOU!

~ Day 1 to a New YOU! ~
Loving You

Like the sky opens after a rainy day
we must open to ourselves....
Learn to love yourself for who you are
and open so the world can see you shine.
~ James Poland

The first step in becoming a new you is loving you. You must learn to love yourself for who you are before you can begin to change. This involves loving your choices, your experiences and any self-perceived imperfections. Once you do, the next step is to believe that you can change and that you are worthy to have the life that you desire. I encourage you to remember and to recognize that change doesn't happen overnight. It is a continual work in progress and should be acknowledged as such.

For many individuals, loving other people and our

animal companions is easy for them. They find it easy to speak the words, "I love you." Some individuals choose to express their affection by simply saying "Take care." These same individuals may find it extremely difficult to love themselves and especially to express it. We tend to only see our self-perceived imperfections rather than seeing ourselves as a beautiful, unique, and miraculous creation.

Loving yourself first (and I don't mean in a selfish way) allows the love you have inside of you to expand outwards. When you open your heart to loving YOU, you will attract this same love back to you because of the Law of Attraction.

In order to attract the love that you desire from another individual, it is important that you love yourself freely and fully. See yourself as the Divine sees you—a beautiful, unique and miraculous creation. There is no one else like you nor will there ever be. When you really love yourself and open your heart to love, you will attract this same love back into your life. Know that you are worthy to have a partner who is worthy to have you!

Wearing a rose quartz bracelet or pendant or carrying a chunk of rose quartz in your pocket is a tangible reminder of this love. Rose quartz is the stone of unconditional love and infinite peace representing both physical and universal love.

Loving YOU exercise

Practice expressing verbally love for YOU. Look in a mirror and tell yourself, "I love you." You can do this in the morning when you are brushing your teeth and combing your hair. It's important for you to mean it. Allow yourself to truly feel the love you have inside of yourself. This exercise will make you smile. It may even make you laugh especially with your first attempt. Laughter is healing. You may feel emotional as well. Allow yourself to feel what you are feeling. There is no shame in crying when doing this exercise, and tears are cleansing. Cross your arms and wrap them around you giving yourself a hug! Breathe in deeply and exhale. All is well.

Questions to Consider

1. When expressing love for others, I find it easy / challenging.

2. When expressing love for others, I feel _____.

3. When expressing love for myself, I find it easy / challenging.

4. When expressing love for myself, I feel _____.

5. When doing the loving you exercise for the first time, the emotions I experienced were _____.

Affirmation to Assist You

Affirm ~ My heart overflows with gratitude and joy. I am conscious of being present in this moment. I recognize that I am love and I am loved. I am allowing myself to simply breathe.

Message to Uplift

Message for today ~ **Romance**

My interpretation ~ The angels are acknowledging romance. Love is in the air. Can you feel it? Love yourself freely and fully and you will attract this same love back into your life.

Note: If today's message does not resonate with you, please practice discernment and choose not to accept it for yourself. I encourage you to go within to interpret the meaning of the messages for you specifically.

~ Day 2 to a New YOU! ~
Choosing Change

Answering the BIG question

Do you desire change in your life?

Is there a particular area you would like change to occur?

Career?

Relationships?

Finances?

Health?

Well-being?

A complete total makeover?

If you have answered yes to any of these questions, you recognize that you are choosing change. Now, it is necessary to acknowledge and identify exactly what aspect(s) of your life that you wish to change.

> *If you don't like something change it;*
> *if you can't change it,*
> *change the way you think about it.*
> ~ *Mary Engelbreit*

I encourage you to do a mini life review and assess how you feel. Take a moment to write down what you "like" and what you "don't like" about your life. I am putting these words in quotes because this determination is based solely on your perception. A thought becomes tangible once it is written on paper. It takes form. You can see the words and touch the paper. Read what you have written and see how you feel when reading it. Acknowledge and recognize the lists you have created with your likes and dislikes.

Be honest with yourself. Do not allow another individual to influence what you choose to change. I commend you for taking action, and I urge you to allow yourself to be present. Breathe in deeply and visualize yourself exhaling what you choose to change. It is time to quit existing and start living! This is your life to live – it's time to live it!

Questions to Consider

Career?

When assessing and reviewing my career choices, I feel _____.

How does your body react?

What is your body telling you?

Do you become emotional as you read what you have written?

Relationships?

When assessing and reviewing my past and current relationships, I feel _____.

How does your body react?

What is your body telling you?

Do you become emotional as you read what you have written?

Finances?

When assessing and reviewing my financial situation, I feel _____.

How does your body react?

What is your body telling you?

Do you become emotional as you read what you have written?

Health?

When assessing and reviewing my health, I feel
_____.

How does your body react?

What is your body telling you?

Do you become emotional as you read what you have written?

Well-being?

When assessing and reviewing my well-being, I feel
_____.

How does your body react?

What is your body telling you?

Do you become emotional as you read what you have written?

A complete total makeover?

When assessing and reviewing my life as it is now, I feel _____.

How does your body react?

What is your body telling you?

Do you become emotional as you read what you have written?

Message to Uplift

Message for today ~ **Soul mate**

My interpretation ~ The angels are acknowledging your soul mate. Soul mates may be friends or family members and you may have multiple soul mates throughout your lifetime. Soul mates are intended to offer you opportunities for learning and growth.

Note: If today's message does not resonate with you, please practice discernment and choose not to accept it for yourself. I encourage you to go within to interpret the meaning of the messages for you specifically.

~ Day 3 to a New YOU! ~
Law of Attraction

What we are today
comes from our thoughts of yesterday,
and our present thoughts
build our life of tomorrow:
Our life is the creation of our mind.
~ Buddha

The Universal Law of Attraction is a tool for manifesting. It is based on the idea that whatever we give a lot of attention to will become part of our lives. In doing so, you are co-creating with the Universe. What you focus on becomes your reality so it is very important to pay attention to your thoughts, words, and actions. If you are guided to do so, I encourage you to learn more about the Law of Attraction from credible sources.

In order to use the Law of Attraction effectively and efficiently, it is imperative that you clearly identify what you want, focus your thoughts on what you have identified, and then allow it to manifest. In other words, do not block the manifestation from occurring by infusing it with doubt, worry, and fear. Trust and have faith that all is as it should be in each and every moment. Also, take into consideration that you will attract what you desire if it is for your highest and best good. Release the need to control the details of the manifestation process such as the how, when, why, what, and where of it. Believe it, live it and you will manifest it if you are intended to. I invite you to envision the reality you desire.

I firmly believe that utilizing a vision or dream board facilitates in the manifestation process especially if you are not a visual thinker. Creating a vision or dream board is a wonderful way to turn thoughts into pictures. You can flip through old magazines and cut out pictures or even search images on the Internet and print them off. Include any words, phrases, and quotes that resonate with you. Glue or tape the images and words to cardboard or poster board and hang them in a location that you will see throughout the day. Feel free to add or remove words and images whenever you are guided to as well. This is your creation; you are only limited by your imagination.

Remember to focus your attention on what you wish to manifest. Do NOT focus on what you already have that you don't like. You are going to manifest what you are focusing on. For example, an individual may desire money to pay bills. Many times, the energy is focused on the bills, which sends the message to the

Universe that you want more bills. If you wish to increase your abundance in your life, focus on abundance and affirming that your needs are met. Do not focus on the bills you receive in the mail. This is very important! Expressing your gratitude for what you already have is equally important.

Listen to the words you utter daily. Word modification may be necessary. Express what you desire rather than your present state of be-ing. Be clear about what you mean. Avoid using the words trying or hoping when declaring what you want as it evokes doubt. Leave it out of the sentence completely. Use the words I AM whenever possible as it is a declaration of what you desire.

I wish to remind you that becoming aware of the words you are using takes time and lots of practice. Listening to other individuals is much easier. I suggest that you really listen when others are speaking and pay attention to their word choices. It will assist you in becoming more aware of your own vocabulary. Words are energy and have a vibration. Choose to use high-vibration words rather than low-vibration words so that you will attract the outcome you desire.

Word Modification Exercise

Practice being aware of the words you speak and write. This takes practice. You may choose to practice by typing or writing the words you are speaking. Look at what you have typed or written. Can you say the same thing in another, more positive life-affirming way? More than likely, you can!

Examples of word modification

Rather than saying ~ *I am unemployed*
Choose to say ~ *I am seeking employment*

Rather than saying ~ *I am sick*
Choose to say ~ *I am taking care of myself*
so that I am healthy

Rather than saying ~ *I am broke*
Choose to say ~ *I am creating an income*
so that my needs are met

Rather than saying ~ *I am cautious of my words*
Choose to say ~ *I am mindful of my words*

Questions to Consider

1. When utilizing the Law of Attraction, I recognize I am attracting _____ because that is what I am focusing on.

2. In reality, I wish to attract _____.

3. When assessing and reviewing my vocabulary, I recognize that I tend to use the following words repeatedly _____.

4. When assessing and reviewing my vocabulary, I recognize that I can modify my vocabulary to actively use the following words more effectively _____.

5. I typically say _____.

6. I will now say _____.

Affirmation to Assist You

Affirm ~ My heart overflows with gratitude and joy. I am conscious of being present in this moment. I recognize that I am a creator, and I am creating my reality. I am allowing myself to simply breathe. I am surrendering to the Universe anything and anyone that no longer serves me or my Higher purpose. I am releasing it now fully and completely. I choose to create my life and all of its experiences consciously.

Message to Uplift

Message for today ~ **Focus**

My interpretation ~ The angels are reminding you to focus. Focus your attention on accomplishing one task at a time and all will be completed.

Note: If today's message does not resonate with you, please practice discernment and choose not to accept it for yourself. I encourage you to go within to interpret the meaning of the messages for you specifically.

~ Day 4 to a New YOU! ~
Identifying Your Desires

*The thing that is really hard, and really amazing,
is giving up on being perfect and
beginning the work of becoming yourself.*
~ Anna Quindlen

Now that you have acknowledged, recognized, and identified exactly what aspect(s) of your life that you desire to change, it is now time to express what you truly desire. Be honest with yourself. Allow yourself the opportunity to express what you really want to do. Answer these questions without thinking or letting your human-ness influence your answers:

My Spirit loves _____.

If I were not afraid, I would _____.

What are you passionate about? What makes your

heart sing? It is okay to change your mind. Know that it is never too late to change your mind or make new choices. Remember, this is your human life experience. This is your reality. No one can live your life for you. They can offer advice and suggestions, but ultimately you should trust what feels right for you.

Take a moment to write down your desires, your dreams, and your aspirations on a piece of paper. You are worthy to receive and to achieve all that you desire. As I previously stated, a thought becomes tangible once it is written on paper. It takes form. You can see the words and touch the paper. Read what you have written and see how you feel when reading it.

You may choose to express your desires and intentions creatively. As I mentioned previously, creating a vision or dream board is a wonderful way to turn thoughts into words and pictures. The images and words you have chosen reflect your dreams so dream big! Your imagination is truly the limit; otherwise, you have no boundaries.

Questions to Consider

1. What do you desire?

How does your body react?

What is it telling you?

Do you become emotional as you read what you have written?

2. What do you wish to manifest?

How does your body react?

What is it telling you?

Do you become emotional as you read what you have written?

3. What do you wish to achieve?

How does your body react?

What is it telling you?

Do you become emotional as you read what you have written?

4. When assessing and reviewing my desires, I find it easy / difficult to list my desires.

5. When reviewing and assessing my desires, I feel _____.

Message to Uplift

Message for today ~ **Ideas & Inspiration**

My interpretation ~ The angels are acknowledging ideas and inspiration. Pay attention to the ideas you receive. You may not know the how, when, why, what and where of the guidance. Nevertheless, you should acknowledge it and express your gratitude for receiving it.

Note: If today's message does not resonate with you, please practice discernment and choose not to accept it for yourself. I encourage you to go within to interpret the meaning of the messages for you specifically.

~ Day 5 to a New YOU! ~
Being Present

If you worry about what might be,
and wonder what might have been,
you will ignore what is.
~ Author Unknown

The word *present* can be defined in two ways: "being in a certain place," and "happening now." I am going to integrate these meanings to convey the message I intend for you to receive. Your mind, body, and Spirit should be unified in one specific physical place right now in order to be fully present.

Being present involves living in the moment rather than focusing on the future or dwelling in the past. Focus on living, be-ing and breathing in the moment. Release and let go of anything and everything that no longer serves you. The past is in the past and cannot be changed. The future has yet to be created so all you have is this present moment. I encourage you to allow yourself the opportunity to be present – right here, right now in this moment. Silence the mind chatter and be at peace.

You are right where you are supposed to be. Yes, I realize that this may be somewhat difficult to understand based on your current life circumstances, but our Spirit knows. Do you have feelings of déjà vu? This is confirmation for you. You are a spiritual being having a human life experience. These experiences include both challenges and triumphs. Both are opportunities for learning and growth. Everything has to do with perception and then your reaction. You can perceive the challenges as the proverbial mountain or the mole-hill. It's up to you. Take each day one day at a time, one moment at a time. Be present in this moment right here right now.

Questions to Consider

1. When assessing and reviewing my current state of being, I tend to dwell in the past / live in the present / focus on the future.

2. When assessing and reviewing my current state of being, I feel _____.

Being present exercise

Focus your energy on being present and in the NOW at this very moment. Be observant and become aware of your surroundings yet allow yourself to simply BE.

What do you see?

What do you feel?

What do you hear?

What do you taste?

What do you think?

Allow yourself to become fully aware and completely present right here right now. Do not allow your mind to wander. Become conscious of this moment. Breathe in deeply and exhale mindfully. Feel your chest expanding as you breathe in and your chest deflating as you exhale. Feel your heart beating rhythmically as blood is coursing through your veins. All you should feel at this moment is being present. Continue being mindful of your breathing and relax. You are present in this moment.

Message to Uplift

Message for today ~ **Study**

My interpretation ~ The angels are reminding you to study. You are always learning and growing. Read the books and take the classes that resonate with you.

Note: If today's message does not resonate with you, please practice discernment and choose not to accept it for yourself. I encourage you to go within to interpret the meaning of the messages for you specifically.

~ Day 6 to a New YOU! ~
Assessing Relationships

Let us be grateful to people who make us happy,
they are the charming gardeners
who make our souls blossom.
~ Marcel Proust

I tell my clients "Hold your heart in your hands and release everything that is not love ~ as love is all there truly is." This statement is a simple reminder to let go of anything and everyone that doesn't come from a place of love. The feelings of fear, anger, resentment, frustration, worry, and jealously serve no purpose in our lives - period.

Throughout our lifetime, we have numerous relationships with many other individuals. These relationships may be labeled as passersby, acquaintances, friends, best friends, and intimate. Family members would also be considered, labeling as immediate and extended family. As the saying goes, people come into our life for a reason, a season or a lifetime. It is not always up to us to determine the reason or the length of a relationship. Of course, we will always be related to family members.

I encourage you to assess the current relationships in your life. Note: There is no need to assess your previous relationships as they are in the past. In doing so, you may choose to allow some relationships to "run their course," so to speak. As you make the conscious effort to maintain healthy relationships and end unhealthy ones (or at least have boundaries), you are taking control of your life. Remember, the Law of Attraction assists in bringing new people into your life as previous relationships come to a close. As far as family members go, you may choose to spend more time with some family members and less time with others.

I encourage you to make the conscious effort to maintain and cultivate those relationships you deem healthy and balanced. In addition, allow yourself the opportunity to observe the relationships that leave you feeling tired and taken advantage of. Remember, no one can make you feel any certain way so it's a good idea to communicate what you are feeling and establish boundaries for yourself. Say "No" when you mean no rather than saying "Yes" because you don't want to hurt someone's feelings. When you say "No," you are saying, "Yes" to yourself!

Relationships (familial, intimate and platonic) allow us

the opportunity to learn and grow from one another. Remember to communicate your needs and desires to yourself and to those people in your life. Speak your truth always and in all ways. You are worthy to have the people in your life who are worthy to have you.

Questions to Consider

1. When assessing my current relationships, I feel _____.

Are they healthy and beneficial or are they draining?

Are they balanced or a bit lop-sided?

Do you tend to be the one maintaining the relationship?

After spending time or chatting on the phone with this person, do you tend to be moody or do you feel joyful?

2. I acknowledge that I have healthy relationships with these individuals _____.

3. I acknowledge that I have unhealthy relationships with these individuals _____.

Affirmation to Assist You

Affirm ~ My heart overflows with gratitude and joy. I am conscious of being present in this moment. I recognize that people may be in my life for a reason, a season or a lifetime. I am allowing myself to simply breathe. I acknowledge and appreciate that when a relationship may end, it is making room for a new relationship to begin.

Message to Uplift

Message for today ~ **Harmony**

My interpretation ~ The angels are acknowledging harmony. Everything is as it should be in each and every moment. All is truly well.

Note: If today's message does not resonate with you, please practice discernment and choose not to accept it for yourself. I encourage you to go within to interpret the meaning of the messages for you specifically.

~ Day 7 to a New YOU! ~
Releasing & Forgiveness

Breathe. Let go. And remind yourself
that this very moment is
the only one you know you have for sure.
~ Oprah Winfrey

Since you have now identified and expressed exactly what aspect(s) of your life that you desire to change; it is time to make a conscious effort to release yourself from your past. Memories and experiences that we have labeled unpleasant tend to remain in our subconscious and even conscious mind. These memories churn and simmer in our minds, resurfacing every now and again.

Individuals tend to replay scenarios over and over again and ask, "What could I have done differently?" or "What if…?" They also play the "should" game saying, "I should have done *this* or I should have done *that*....then *this* would not have happened." How can you be so sure? Hindsight, which is the ability of understanding later what was actually the best thing to do, is formidable. We tend to retain from experiences what is necessary for future growth.

> *Forgive all who have offended you,*
> *not for them, but for yourself.*
> **~ Harriet Nelson**

In addition, I encourage you to forgive yourself just as you would forgive another individual. Forgive yourself of any past choices that you have made and now regret. Every choice you made was absolutely the right choice at the time you made it with the information you had available to you at the time.

Each one of us is having a human experience because we choose to. Learning from our experiences and not repeating them is a benefit to having them to begin with. Do not allow those experiences to define you. Release yourself from the pain, heartache and frustration you have been holding on to. The past is in the past. It cannot be changed. Allow yourself to let go so that you can begin anew! New beginnings start with the release of old thoughts.

Releasing Exercise

This exercise is intended to assist you in letting go of the past and moving forward. Use this exercise to let go of the "stuff" you have been holding on to.

Take a moment to just BE. Sit in a chair with your
back straight and your palms up (open to receiving).
Close your eyes. Allow the memory of an experience
or individual that you have labeled unpleasant to come
into your consciousness. Do not relive the experience
or try to remember the details. Simply allow this
individual, event, or experience to come into your
mind. Then, acknowledge and release this memory
you have labeled unpleasant. Say aloud or in your
mind, "I acknowledge. I release." Breathe in deeply
and visualize yourself exhaling this experience or
individual.

Continue to allow memories of an experience or
individual that you have labeled unpleasant to come
into your mind in order for you to release them. It is
imperative that you do not try to remember the details
of these memories. Simply acknowledge and release
them. Breathe in deeply and visualize yourself
exhaling this experience or individual.

I encourage you to repeat this exercise whenever you
are guided to do so, including those times you may
feel like you are holding on to something from the past
because it does keep coming to the surface. Allow
anything and everything to come to the surface...even
the "little" things. After completing this exercise,
breathe in deeply once again allowing the breath to
revitalize your energy. Visualize that you have
refreshed your be-ing just as you would refresh your
computer screen.

Questions to Consider

1. When reflecting on my thinking, I do / do not tend to replay scenarios in my mind.

2. Prior to doing the releasing exercise, I felt
_____.

2. After doing the releasing exercise, I feel
_____.

Message to Uplift

Message for today ~ **Nature**

My interpretation ~ The angels are acknowledging nature. Spend time outdoors grounding your energy and connecting to Mother Earth. Breathe in the fresh air and be mindful of your breaths. Doing so will refresh and revitalize your energy.

Note: If today's message does not resonate with you, please practice discernment and choose not to accept it for yourself. I encourage you to go within to interpret the meaning of the messages for you specifically.

~ Day 8 to a New YOU! ~
Mind, Body, Spirit as One

We are not human beings having a spiritual experience.
We are spiritual beings having a human experience.
~ Pierre Teilhard de Chardin

Many individuals firmly consider that an object must be tangible in order for it to exist. We must be able to see it and touch it for it to be real. I encourage you to believe that we are more than our physical body. I feel that we must recognize that we are a spiritual being having a human life experience. It is important to cultivate the Spirit, yet equally important to honor the mind and body. Therefore, I encourage you to acknowledge that the mind, body, and Spirit are ONE— a unified entity. Balancing the aspects of mind, body, and Spirit is an integral part of our overall well-being. One's physical health, mental/emotional health and spiritual health should all be considered.

A healthy diet and exercise is necessary for your physical well-being. In essence, you are what you eat. Fresh fruits and vegetables will assist in raising your vibration. In order to be healthy, you must feel healthy. Take a moment to reflect how your body reacts and how you feel after eating certain foods. Processed foods and "fast" foods will typically leave you feeling tired and sluggish. Moderation is essential. Over-indulgence only leads regret and a stomache later. Take note of how your own body feels after consuming certain foods.

Lack of activity destroys the good condition
of every human being,
while movement and methodical physical exercise
save it and preserve it.
*~ **Plato***

I enjoy walking and breathing in the fresh air. Walking is not strenuous exercise, yet it does get the "heart pumping" and the blood circulating if you walk at a brisk pace.

Mental exercises such as memory games, Sudoku, crossword, and word seek puzzles stimulate your brain. As I previously mentioned, assessing the relationships in your life is encouraged. As you make the conscious effort to maintain healthy relationships and end unhealthy ones, you are taking control of your life. In doing so, you are contributing to your mental health.

Take time each day to connect with YOU, your inner self, through meditation. Meditation takes many forms.

It can be sitting quietly, listening to a guided meditation, going for a walk, or spending time outdoors in nature. Be mindful of your breaths as you clear your mind and open your heart two to three times a day for 2-3 minutes at a time. This brief meditative excursion has wondrous results.

Questions to Consider

1. What are you feeling emotionally during this process of transformation?

2. What are you feeling physically during this process of transformation?

3. My diet consists of _____.

4. When assessing and reviewing the foods I eat, I typically feel _____ after eating _____.

5. My daily exercise regime consists of _____.

6. My mental exercises include _____.

7. My form of meditation consists of _____.

8. When meditating and connecting with my inner self, I feel _____.

Message to Uplift

Message for today ~ **Celebration**

My interpretation ~ The angels are acknowledging a celebration. Celebrate being YOU! You are a beautiful, unique and miraculous creation. There is no one else like you nor will there ever be.

Note: If today's message does not resonate with you, please practice discernment and choose not to accept it for yourself. I encourage you to go within to interpret the meaning of the messages for you specifically.

~ Day 9 to a New YOU! ~
Perception

*There is nothing either good or bad,
but thinking makes it so.*
~ ***William Shakespeare***

Perception is how we view or perceive an experience through our senses – sight, taste, touch, smell, and hearing. We may choose to label an experience as good or bad, positive or negative. In reality, this is simply our perception or a personal assessment of the experience.

Changing your perception assists you in changing your life. Remove the constraints of the "box" you have created for yourself, and allow yourself to view experiences from another individual's point of view. A group of people may have all had the exact same experience, but will each perceive the experience differently based on their own perception. It is next to impossible to alter someone's perception. In circumstances that you do not see "eye-to-eye," simply listen and then practice non-attachment to the outcome. This means that you are recognizing what you have heard, but you are not allowing another individual's perception to influence your own.

An example of this would be a group of people having dinner together and then going to an event such as concert. Food preferences and musical tastes vary so the experience will differ for each person.

In addition, I highly recommend that you avoid labeling experiences as much as possible. If you can simply refer to an experience as an experience rather than labeling it as "good" or "bad," you will change the energy of the experience. Of course, we want to bask in the wonderful energy of an AWESOME experience. I am primarily referring to those experiences we prefer not to have again.

I have noticed when working with clients that they typically will not label a wonderful experience. They just start talking about it with joy in their voice. On the other hand, the word "bad" is almost always used to label an experience they didn't enjoy.

Questions to Consider

1. Have you been in a situation with others where you have noticed that you each perceived the experience differently?

2. How did you feel when this occurred?

3. What does your self-talk dialogue sound like?

4. What words do you typically use when describing an experience?

5. Do you find yourself using the words "bad" or "negative" rather than "good" or "positive" when telling others about your experiences?

Message to Uplift

Message for today ~ **Support**

My interpretation ~ The angels are offering you their support. They are unable to intervene in your freewill choices unless it is dire circumstances so you must call upon them when you need assistance. They are standing by ready, willing and able to assist. Call upon your family and friends as well because they might not know you need their help.

Note: If today's message does not resonate with you, please practice discernment and choose not to accept it for yourself. I encourage you to go within to interpret the meaning of the messages for you specifically.

~ Day 10 to a New YOU! ~
Discovering You

Your work is to discover your world
and then with all your heart give yourself to it.
*~ **Buddha***

Now is the time to discover who you really are in this moment. You have acknowledged what you wish to change, identified your desires, and expressed what you wish to achieve. I invite you to live a life of purpose. Your purpose is to be you. The core of your purpose focuses solely on your happiness and well-being. Allow yourself the opportunity to explore, discover, learn and embrace what really makes your heart sing. Know that all is as it should be in each and every moment. Have no regrets and live each day fully and freely. When you come from a place of love and see everything, including yourself, through the eyes of love, love is all that will exist. Reflect on who you were, who you are and who you are becoming.

Discovering you Exercise

Discover who YOU really are. Today is the perfect day to do so and to honor you. Actually, every day is the perfect day to honor you.

What makes your heart sing and your eyes twinkle? Reach down deep inside of you and allow yourself to see that you are perfect in every way. See past the illusions and the self-perceived imperfections and discover the real you – the essence of who you are.

You are BEAUTIFUL! You really are! You are a miraculous creation. There is no one else exactly like you, which makes you unique.

Breathe in deeply feeling the embodiment of who you are. Divine love is truly the only reality. Everything else is simply an illusion that our human-ness creates. Focus your energy on being the best you can possibly be. Focus your energy on seeing that you are a beautiful, unique and miraculous creation.

Questions to Consider

1. Who are you?

2. Why are you here?

3. What are you supposed to be doing?

4. Do you believe that this is all there is?

5. When I think about who I really am, I feel
_____.

6. When I think about what makes my heart sing and my eyes twinkle, I immediately think about
_____.

7. When thinking about this, I feel _____.

Message to Uplift

Message for today ~ **New Beginnings**

My interpretation ~ The angels are acknowledging new beginnings. Each day is a new beginning. Recognize that the past is in the past and cannot be changed. The future is yet to be created. This present moment is all that truly exists.

Note: If today's message does not resonate with you, please practice discernment and choose not to accept it for yourself. I encourage you to go within to interpret the meaning of the messages for you specifically.

~ Day 11 to a New YOU! ~
Paying Attention

Every time you don't follow your inner guidance,
you feel a loss of energy, loss of power,
a sense of spiritual deadness.
~ Shakti Gawain

The next step involves paying attention to the guidance you are receiving. I am referring to the guidance from your Higher Self, your angels, and your guides. Sometimes, this guidance is subtle and comes in whispers and gentle nudges. When we refuse to acknowledge this guidance, it becomes louder, more persistent and may feel like the proverbial push or shove. I feel that it is extremely important to recognize and acknowledge the guidance you are receiving and to give thanks for it. You may not understand the how, when, where, why, or what aspects of the guidance; yet you should acknowledge it and express your gratitude for receiving it. Call upon your angels and guides for clarification of the message as well.

In addition, I encourage you to pay special attention to the messages your body is sending you. Listen to your gut instinct, which is located in your solar plexus chakra. As you become attuned to listening to your body and what it is telling you, it will become easier to recognize the messages that originate from this area. Your physical body is a great device for gauging energy and situations. If something does not feel right, do not proceed. Have you ever felt nauseous or had "butterflies" in your stomach? This may be feelings of nervousness, or it may be your body's way of telling you something.

The term, discern, means to distinguish or perceive clearly. Therefore, practicing discernment is the ability to perceive the messages your Higher Self and body are telling you. Take mental note of this guidance. It is up to you if you choose to listen and to take action on this guidance. You have free will and can always choose.

Recognizing and acknowledging the guidance you are receiving assists you in becoming more aware— more "in tune" with you. Also, pay attention to what I refer to as "chills" or a buzzing sensation. Whenever this occurs, I immediately verbally acknowledge these sensations because I recognize them to be validation from my guides that what I am saying is correct.

As you are guided to throughout the day, find a quiet peaceful place that you can practice listening to the guidance you are receiving. It will be easier to hear when you are not distracted by outside noise. You may choose to meditate briefly or simply be present and listen.

Questions to Consider

1. When assessing and reviewing previous experiences, I recall that I have received guidance and _____.

2. I recall instances when the guidance was subtle, but became more persistent when I ignored it. During that instance, I _____.

3. When you are in certain situations or around certain people, do you sometimes feel uneasy and want to leave?

4. Did you resist this feeling and decide to stay, causing you to go against your inner guidance?

5. When I assessed that experience, I remember _____.

6. Do you recall feeling nauseous or having "butterflies" in your stomach?

7. When I assessed that experience, I remember
_____.

8. I am familiar with discernment and I use it on occasion / regularly.

Message to Uplift

Message for today ~ **Divine Guidance**

My interpretation ~ The angels are acknowledging Divine guidance. Yes, the guidance you are receiving is Divinely guided. You may not know the how, when, what, why or where aspects of the guidance, but you should acknowledge it and express your gratitude for receiving it.

Note: If today's message does not resonate with you, please practice discernment and choose not to accept it for yourself. I encourage you to go within to interpret the meaning of the messages for you specifically.

~ Day 12 to a New YOU! ~
Living in the Present

With the past, I have nothing to do; nor with the future.
I live now.
~ Ralph Waldo Emerson

It is time to let go of the past, live in the present, and look to the future for it is this attitude that will transform you. The past is in the past; it cannot be changed. It is nice to look to the future, but you don't want to miss out on the present in doing so.

In essence, all you have is this present moment in time. The past no longer exists and the future has yet to be created. All you have are memories of the past and dreams and aspirations for the future.

The concept of time is a matter of perspective. The Universe operates on Divine time whereas humans function on linear time with clocks and calendars.

There is a difference. When you focus your energy on living in the present, the more relaxed and at ease you will be spiritually and emotionally speaking. I encourage you to acknowledge your previous experiences and continue to make those future plans, but don't allow the past or future to consume you. Focus on living, be-ing and breathing in this present moment.

Have you made plans with someone and then they had to cancel or you were unable to attend? How did this make you feel? Did you become upset or were you at peace? Your reaction to the situation offers you the ability to see if you are actually living in the present time. When you recognize that circumstances may arise and you choose to not allow it to affect you emotionally, then you are living in the present. Yes, you may be disappointed, but does this disappointment or frustration consume you? Stuff happens that are beyond our control. We can only control our reaction.

You are always where you are supposed to be in each and every moment. Regardless of what your humanness questions, you are doing what you are supposed to be doing. Allow yourself to be present in this moment right here right now. The past no longer exists except for in memories, and the future has yet to be created except for in our hopes and dreams. The more that you focus on this moment and trust that each choice you are making is the right choice— the more you will understand this concept.

Questions to Consider

1. I find myself reflecting on the past less often / more often.

2. Why?

3. I find myself looking to the future less often / more often.

4. Why?

5. I find myself living in the present less often / more often.

6. Why?

Message to Uplift

Message for today ~ **Serenity**

My interpretation ~ The angels are acknowledging serenity. Feel the peace, love, joy and happiness. All is truly well.

Note: If today's message does not resonate with you, please practice discernment and choose not to accept it for yourself. I encourage you to go within to interpret the meaning of the messages for you specifically.

~ Day 13 to a New YOU! ~
Awareness

Awareness is the key to transformation.
*~ **Eckhart Tolle***

Awareness involves both consciousness and cognizance. This includes being cognizant of our surroundings and the people coming into and leaving our life. The Universe will assist us in bringing people, teachers and experiences into our awareness so that we can learn, heal and grow from them.

For myself, I have noticed that certain people will come into my awareness at exactly the right time for me to receive a message. The message may not be directed specifically towards me, but I receive it loud and clear nonetheless. I can almost feel a switch being turned on and off enabling me to glean exactly what I need. I recognize these as opportunities for learning and growth for myself.

Let us not look back in anger,
nor forward in fear,
but around in awareness.
~ James Thurber

Songs on the radio, television commercials, and even upcoming events are worth paying attention to especially if you keep seeing or hearing about them repeatedly. Check in with yourself and assess if there is an underlying message or if you are intended to take it literally. Symbols are everywhere. Our perception assists us in our individual interpretation of these symbols. A symbol may mean one thing to an individual and something entirely different to another individual. Practicing discernment and what feels right to you is essential.

Awareness Exercise

Increase your awareness level by focusing and tuning in with each of your five senses. Spend time each day being cognizant of your surroundings. Make notes in your journal of your experiences as you are guided to do so.

What do you hear?

What do you see?

What do you taste?

What do you smell?

What do you feel?

As you become accustomed to paying attention, it will be easier to notice when you are not distracted. Silence your mind chatter and sit in quiet repose. Take note of the guidance you are receiving and the signs you are observing. Remember that these signs may be in the form of cloud formations, found in nature such as birds or butterflies, songs on the radio, overhead conversations, etc. Do not second-guess if you are actually receiving a sign. You may not understand the meaning of the sign at the moment you receive it. Simply acknowledge it, express your gratitude for it and you will understand the meaning of the sign when you are supposed to.

Affirmation to Assist You

Affirm ~ My heart overflows with gratitude and joy. I am conscious of being present in this moment. I recognize the guidance I am receiving. I am allowing myself to simply breathe. I acknowledge and appreciate that I am not alone for my angels and guides are with me always.

Questions to Consider

1. How would you assess your awareness level?

2. Are you adept at picking up on cues?

3. Do you tend to look for the underlying message, also known as "reading between the lines?"

4. Do you tend to interpret messages at face-value only?

Message to Uplift

Message for today ~ **Miracles**

My interpretation ~ The angels are acknowledging miracles. Every moment is a miracle. Every breath of life is a miracle. Choose to view everything as a miracle or nothing as a miracle.

Note: If today's message does not resonate with you, please practice discernment and choose not to accept it for yourself. I encourage you to go within to interpret the meaning of the messages for you specifically.

~ Day 14 to a New YOU! ~
Expressing Gratitude

If you want to turn your life around, try thankfulness.
It will change your life mightily.
~ Gerald Good

Gratitude is an expression of thankfulness. The simple words, "Thank you," extend far beyond their utterance. They are an acknowledgement of appreciation. Thanking another individual for having completed a task, the extension of a hand in friendship, and even the recognition of a compliment reflect the gratitude you are feeling. The energy of gratitude is a high vibration and one of love. The Universe will reflect this grateful energy back to you in the form of blessings.

As we express our gratitude,
we must never forget that the highest appreciation
is not to utter words, but to live by them.
~ John Fitzgerald Kennedy

In addition to speaking your gratitude, I believe it should also be illustrated in your actions. I encourage you to acknowledge and express what which you are thankful for as it will assist you in your transformation. By expressing gratitude, we remind ourselves of what we do have rather than focusing solely on our desires.

I express my own gratitude daily saying, "I am so grateful for my family and friends, my angels and guides, and most of all, for my own blessed life. I am thankful for those individuals who have come into my life, the opportunities I have available to me, and the experiences I have had."

Questions to Consider

1. What are you thankful for?

2. When do you express your gratitude?

3. How do you express your gratitude?

Message to Uplift

Message for today ~ **Archangel Michael**

My interpretation ~ The angels are acknowledging Archangel Michael. Call upon Michael for strength, courage and protection. You are not alone.

Note: If today's message does not resonate with you, please practice discernment and choose not to accept it for yourself. I encourage you to go within to interpret the meaning of the messages for you specifically.

~ Day 15 to a New YOU! ~
Trusting in the Process

Trust is letting go of needing to know all the details
before you open your heart.
~ Author Unknown

According to the Webster Dictionary, trust is defined as a "strong reliance on the integrity, honest, dependability, etc. of some person or thing; having confidence and faith." Trusting in the process means to have confidence in the process and to have confidence in yourself. You are permitting yourself to do something without fear of the outcome. You are going full-steam ahead knowing that this is your life to live. You are living a life of purpose— to be YOU!

Trust that everything is happening when and if it is supposed to. The Universe doesn't function on human's linear time; it operates on Divine time. Breathe in deeply green healing energy from

Archangel Raphael and exhale any worries, concerns, doubt and fear you may be experiencing pertaining to the process. It is time to let go and simply TRUST that all is as it should be in each and every moment! Allow yourself the opportunity to be present, to be in the flow and to trust.

I am always doing that which I cannot do,
in order that I may learn how to do it.
~ Pablo Picasso

Fear and worry serve no purpose other than creating more fear and worry. They go hand and hand inhibiting and creating blockages in our life. Fear tends to suppress living because we avoid taking risks in life. We are fearful of the outcome or what others may think of us so we avoid taking the risk altogether. Have the courage to create the life that you desire. Take a moment to reflect. Have your desires changed?

Questions to Consider

1. If I were not afraid, I would _____

2. I typically do / do not find that I am able to trust.

3. Are you able to trust individuals?

4. Are you able to trust in the outcome of your experiences?

5. When reviewing and assessing my desires, I feel _____.

6. What do you desire?

7. What do you wish to manifest?

8. What do you wish to achieve?

Message to Uplift

Message for today ~ **Retreat**

My interpretation ~ The angels are acknowledging a retreat. There is no need to travel far. You can simply go within.

Note: If today's message does not resonate with you, please practice discernment and choose not to accept it for yourself. I encourage you to go within to interpret the meaning of the messages for you specifically.

~ Day 16 to a New YOU! ~
Ground, Center & Protect Your Energy

Nowhere can man find a quieter
or more untroubled retreat
than in his own soul.
~ Marcus Aurelius

As spiritual energetic beings having our own human life experience, it is important to ground, center and protect our personal energy. Grounding your energy keeps you present, in the moment and completes the energy circuit. Keeping firmly planted helps prevent feelings of fuzziness or spacey-ness that can often disburse your personal energy. Visualize energy passing from the root chakra to the center of the Earth, or roots sprouting from the bottom of the feet.

I like to visualize my feet being connected to the Earth as if I was a tree being rooted to the ground. Intention is the key! You may also feel inclined to ground yourself at different times throughout the day. Crystals such as hematite, tourmaline, and smoky quartz work well too. Not only do these crystals assist in grounding and protecting one's energy, but they also dissolve negativity and harmonize the mind, body, and spirit.

You can also ground your energy by visualizing the Earth having a huge white heart of light in the center of it. Visualize an anchor of white light coming from your heart to the Earth's heart grounding you in love and light.

Protecting, also known as shielding, is necessary to keep yourself protected from another individual's "stuff" and helps keep personal energy separated. Visualizing a white light or a bubble surrounding you will help protect and shield you. Use whatever visualization feels most comfortable and resonates best with your energy at the time. Only love can penetrate this bubble of light, everything else will be dispelled and fall way.

I personally like to visualize a white light surrounding my body. You can get creative and layer colors such as pink, yellow, blue, green, violet, white, etc. surrounding you and it can be as big as you want (even 8 feet around you or larger).

Centering involves finding that calm spot deep inside yourself that is eternal being-ness. I like to visualize a white ball of light at my core in stomach area. Take a few deep breaths and bring awareness inward to the central essence - that place that is peaceful and serene no matter what the external circumstance.

Remember to ground, protect and center your energy daily. We are all of the same energy, but we are each having our own life experiences.

Grounding Exercise

Envision tree roots coming up through your feet and a vine wrapping around your legs. This vine is extending upwards into your root chakra, moving up into your sacral chakra, moving up and extending into your solar plexus chakra and resting in your heart chakra grounding you to Mother Earth. Now, envision white light from Source consciousness coming in through your crown chakra, down into your third eye chakra, down into your throat chakra, and meeting with Mother Earth energy at your heart chakra. You are grounded to Earth and to Light.

Questions to Consider

1. Prior to grounding my energy, I felt _____.

2. After grounding my energy, I feel _____.

3. Prior to intentionally shielding, I felt _____.

4. After shielding my energy, I feel _____.

5. Prior to centering my energy, I felt _____.

6. After centering my energy, I feel _____.

Message to Uplift

Message for today ~ **Surrender & Release**

My interpretation ~ The angels are reminding you to surrender and release. Surrender to the Universe anyone and anything that no longer serves you or your Higher Purpose. Release them so you can move forward with grace and ease.

Note: If today's message does not resonate with you, please practice discernment and choose not to accept it for yourself. I encourage you to go within to interpret the meaning of the messages for you specifically.

~ Day 17 to a New YOU! ~
Honoring Beliefs

Let the world know you as you are,
not as you think you should be,
because sooner or later, if you are posing,
you will forget the pose,
and then where are you?
~ Fanny Brice

Honor and respect your beliefs as well as other individual's beliefs. Identifying and honoring your personal beliefs is necessary, but it is equally important to acknowledge that not everyone has the same belief system as you. Having the courage to express your beliefs to others and not being afraid of what they might think involves fortitude. Allowing yourself to be who you really are with all people requires that you stand in your power. Standing in your power simply means "owning" what you believe to be true. Emanating this power in your words and actions requires no effort or thought when you allow yourself to just BE. It definitely does take courage to be your authentic self while being true to you.

Most people tend to avoid discussions about politics and religion because they are deemed sensitive topics to discuss. Personally, I enjoy discussing both topics even though they tend to become very opinionated. I recognize that my opinion may be the minority opinion in a group rather than the majority, but it is healthy to have the confidence to express one's opinion.

From my perspective, I believe that there is a time and place to express your thoughts and attitudes in regards to a particular subject matter especially when you haven't been asked for them. In my opinion, sometimes it is best to observe, allow and let go rather than becoming consumed with the energy that may arise. You are honoring your beliefs, but are choosing not to express them verbally. The choice is ultimately yours to make.

Questions to Consider

1. I find it easy / difficult to honor and respect my beliefs.

2. What are some of your personal beliefs?

3. What are some of your personal beliefs that you recognize as differing from others' beliefs?

4. How do you feel when you acknowledge this?

5. I find it hard to discuss these topics _____.

6. Why?

7. I find it easy to discuss these topics _____.

8. Why?

Message to Uplift

Message for today ~ **Children**

My interpretation ~ The angels are acknowledging children. Nurture your inner child just as you would your children— both human and furry!

Note: If today's message does not resonate with you, please practice discernment and choose not to accept it for yourself. I encourage you to go within to interpret the meaning of the messages for you specifically.

~ Day 18 to a New YOU! ~
Standing in Your Power

*It takes courage to grow up
and become who you really are.*
~ e.e. cummings

Allowing yourself to be who you really are with all people all of the time requires that you stand in your power. This involves communicating your needs and desires to others as well as to yourself. Standing in your power simply means "owning" what you believe to be true and then speaking your truth. Emanating this power in your words and actions requires no thought when you become accustomed to doing so.

*When you live in reaction, you give your power away.
Then, you get to experience what you gave you power to.*
~ N. Smith

Throughout your life, some people may try to control you or the choices you are making. When you allow this to happen, you are either consciously or subconsciously giving your power away to another. Do you recognize when this happens? How does it make you feel?

It's time for you to stand up, speak your truth and stand in your power. As I have stated before, every experience offers an opportunity for learning and growth. Your perception and then your reaction to the experience will determine the ultimate outcome of the experience.

Anytime a pattern or experience repeats itself, it is important to acknowledge it and then allow yourself to see things from a higher perspective. These experiences will continue to repeat themselves until you get the lesson the experience is offering. You may ask, "What am I supposed to learn from this experience? Why do I feel this way?"

Too often we underestimate the power of a touch,
a smile, a kind word, a listening ear,
an honest compliment, or the smallest act of caring,
all of which have the potential to turn a life around.
~ Leo Buscaglia

Know that you are making a difference in the lives of others by simply being YOU. No extra work is required. By setting an example and standing in your power, you allow others to do the same. Do not doubt the power that you hold within. In other words, quit doubting your ability to make a difference.

Smiling, offering a kind word to another, and holding

the door open are effortless acts that have meaningful results. Both the recipient and the giver walk away from the interaction feeling lighter and loved. No gesture is too small nor goes unnoticed. Simply sharing a smile or offering a kind word will not only raise the recipient's vibration, but will also raise your vibration, as the giver or sender, as well. Practice compassion with everyone you come into contact with including passersby in the store. Smile and say, "Hello!" It's really easy to do and both individuals will feel lighter and shine their own lights brighter!

Questions to Consider

1. What do you feel when you read the words, "standing in your power?"

2. When reviewing and assessing your life, do you feel like you are currently standing in your power?

3. How would you assess your overall interaction with other individuals?

4. Do you recall an experience when you allowed someone to take your power away?

5. How did it feel when that occurred?

Affirmation to Assist You

Affirm ~ I recognize that I am not the same person I was yesterday nor will I be the same person tomorrow that I am today. My Spirit is continually healing and growing. I recognize my power as I tap into my inner knowingness. I trust in the process as it unfolds.

Message to Uplift

Message for today ~ **Blessings**

My interpretation ~ The angels are showering you with blessings. Open your arms wide to receive these blessings. Know that you are worthy to receive these blessings as well.

Note: If today's message does not resonate with you, please practice discernment and choose not to accept it for yourself. I encourage you to go within to interpret the meaning of the messages for you specifically.

~ Day 19 to a New YOU! ~
All About Chakras

Focusing on the act of breathing clears the mind
of all daily distractions and clears our energy,
enabling us to better connect with the Spirit within.
~ Author Unknown

Chakras are spinning wheels of light that act as energy transformers. They take the life force that is all around us and transform it into the various frequencies we need bringing them into our subtle energy system. Chakras are shaped like the circular motion of water flowing down a drain.

In addition to the major chakras, minor chakras are in the hands, feet, knees and other parts of the body. Each chakra extends out from the spine with the front side generally involved with receiving subtle energy and the backside is generally involved with sending energy out, although it is possible for the direction to change back and forth from time to time.

Clearing and balancing your chakras is an easy task to accomplish. Doing so clears the energetic clutter, so to speak, and revitalizes your energy. As you become more adept at visualizing the chakras and their associated colors, you may choose to do this in the shower just as I do. As the water cleanses my physical body, I am clearing and balancing my energetic body.

I am offering you a quick and effective exercise to assist you in clearing and balancing your chakras. Please know that you can do this exercise whenever you feel guided to. You may choose to do it daily as you take time for YOU!

Chakras Explained

1. **The Root**, also known as the Base, chakra is red and is located at the bottom of the torso near the tip of the tailbone. The energy the root chakra supplies creates the will to live and is involved with our need for food, shelter, clothing, and the basic necessities of life.

2. **The Sacral** chakra is orange and is located just above the pubic bone. The sacral chakra supplies energy for sexuality, reproduction, the enjoyment of life, and the physical attraction in relationships. It is also one of the areas where guilt is hidden.

3. **The Solar Plexus** chakra is yellow and is located just below the sternum, near the diaphragm. The solar

plexus chakra is involved with self-expression, taking action in the world, confidence, and personal power. It can also be a place where fear and anger is held. This is your "gut instinct."

4. **The Heart** chakra is green and is located in the center of the chest. The heart chakra supplies energy for all aspects of love, joy, compassion, and surrender. It supplies all parts of the energy field with nurturing and can be a source of spiritual connection and guidance.

5. **The Throat** chakra is blue and is located in the throat area. It supplies energy for speaking, thinking, communicating, writing, and creative expression. The throat chakra can also be involved with clairaudience, contemplation, and inner guidance. It is one pathway through which our feelings are expressed.

6. **The Third Eye** chakra is indigo or purple and is located between the eyebrows. The third eye chakra supplies energy for self-awareness, higher consciousness, clairvoyance, inner vision, conceptual thinking, planning, and insight. In mediation, the third eye is a pathway to higher dimensions and higher consciousness.

7. **The Crown** chakra is white and is located at the top of the head and points upward. The crown chakra's energy connects with the spiritual realms including higher consciousness and the Higher Power. It is one of the pathways to enlightenment.

Clearing and Balancing Chakra Exercise

Take a moment to just BE. Sit in a chair with your back straight and your palms up open to receiving. Close your eyes. Relax. Breathe in deeply and exhale. You may want to visualize the chakras and their corresponding colors as fruits, vegetables, or even flowers.

Begin with the root chakra ~ This is your area of survival needs and where the lower energies of fear, doubt, worry, anger, and frustration reside. Visualize it as red, beautiful, healthy, balanced and cleared. Breathe in deeply green healing energy from Archangel Raphael and exhale anything and anyone that no longer serves you.

Move up to the sacral chakra ~ This is your area of creativity. Visualize it as orange, beautiful, healthy, balanced and cleared. Breathe in deeply green healing energy from Archangel Raphael and exhale anything and anyone that no longer serves you.

Move up to the solar plexus chakra ~ This is your gut instinct. Visualize it as yellow, beautiful, healthy, balanced and cleared. Breathe in deeply green healing energy from Archangel Raphael and exhale anything and anyone that no longer serves you.

Move up to the heart chakra ~ Allow your chest to expand and your heart to open fully to receive the love that is all around you. Visualize it as green, beautiful, healthy, balanced and cleared. Breathe in deeply green healing energy from Archangel Raphael. Allow this energy to fill your lungs and your heart and flow through your veins. Exhale anything and anyone that no longer serves you.

Move up to the throat chakra ~ This is your voice and your area of communication. Allow yourself to communicate your needs and desires to yourself and to others. Visualize it as blue, beautiful, healthy, balanced and cleared. Breathe in deeply green healing energy from Archangel Raphael and exhale anything and anyone that no longer serves you.

Move up to the third eye chakra ~ This is your area of psychic awareness. Visualize it as indigo, beautiful, healthy, balanced and cleared. Breathe in deeply green healing energy from Archangel Raphael and exhale anything and anyone that no longer serves you.

And lastly, you are at the crown chakra... your connection to Source, The Higher Power, All That Is ~ Visualize it as pure white light, beautiful, healthy, balanced and cleared. Breathe in deeply green healing energy from Archangel Raphael and exhale anything and anyone that no longer serves you.

Once again, breathe in deeply the healing energy and exhale your pain, worry, fear, frustration, anger, and anything and everything that no longer serves you. Release and let it go! You chakras have been cleared and balanced. You are love and you are loved and so it is.

Questions to Consider

1. Prior to clearing and balancing chakra exercise, I felt _____.

2. After the clearing and balancing chakra exercise, I feel _____.

Working with Crystals

You may also be guided to work with crystals to clear and balance your chakras. Choose crystals associated with each of the chakras and their associated colors. Place the crystals on the corresponding chakra while you are lying flat. Breathe in deeply and exhale several times as you visualize your chakras being cleared and balanced.

My favorite crystals for this purpose include:

1. **Root** (Red) ~ Smoky Quartz
Dissipates negativity. Balances energies of mind and body. Protective and grounding.

2. **Sacral** (Orange) ~ Carnelian Agate
Perception, precision. Increases physical energy. Protection against emotions of fear and anger.

3. **Solar Plexus** (Yellow) ~ Citrine
Enhances body's healing energy. Good for mental focus, endurance, optimism, and self-esteem.

4. **Heart** (Green) ~ Aventurine
Creativity, motivation, leadership. Stone of good luck.
Balances male-female energies.

5. **Throat** (Blue) ~ Blue Lace Agate
Spirituality, grace, inspiration, inner attunement.

6. **Third Eye** (Indigo) ~ Amethyst
Enhances psychic abilities. Sedative, protective,
contentment. Stone of peace and strength.

7. **Crown** (White/Violet) ~ Clear Quartz
Receives, activates, stores, transmits, and amplifies
energy. Brings harmony to the soul.

Message to Uplift

Message for today ~ **Body Care**

My interpretation ~ The angels are acknowledging
body care. Choose to see past any self-perceived
imperfections and love your physical body. Remember
to exercise, stay hydrated, be mindful of your dietary
intake, and rest when you need to.

Note: If today's message does not resonate with you,
please practice discernment and choose not to accept it
for yourself. I encourage you to go within to interpret
the meaning of the messages for you specifically.

~ Day 20 to a New YOU! ~
Tuning In

*You have to leave the city of your comfort
and go into the wilderness of your intuition.
What you'll discover will be wonderful.
What you'll discover is yourself.*
~ **Alan Alda**

Pay attention to the messages your body is sending you. Listen to your gut instinct, which is located in your solar plexus chakra. Your body is a great device for gauging energy and situations. If something doesn't feel right to you, don't proceed.

As I mentioned previously, the guidance may be a subtle whisper or a gentle nudge. Other times, the guidance may become louder and more persistent (think of the proverbial 2 x 4). Recognizing and acknowledging the guidance you are receiving assists you in becoming more aware— more "in tune" with you.

As you become attuned to listening to your body and what it is telling you, it will become easier to recognize the messages that originate from this area. Find a quiet peaceful place that you can practice listening to the guidance you are receiving. It will be easier to "hear" when you are not distracted by outside noise.

I like to "check in" with myself especially when I am making a decision. To do so, I connect with my inner self, and then I pay attention to how I am feeling. Your gut instinct will never let you down. However, I also recommend gauging the rest of your body as well. I experience stress as shoulder tension and headaches. Breathing in deeply and exhaling allows me to release the tension and stress. I have the tendency to "sigh" when I feel this way. I recognize that I am doing it so I make a concerted to effort to blow rather than just sigh when I am exhaling.

Questions to Consider

1. When assessing and reviewing experiences from the past week, I recall that I have received guidance on these occasions: _____.

2. I acknowledge that I have become more / less attuned to listening to my body and the messages it is telling me.

3. What has your body been telling you?

4. When I am stressed, I feel stress in these areas of my body _____ .

5. To cope with feeling stressed, I _____ .

6. To alleviate stress, I _____ .

Message to Uplift

Message for today ~ **Emerging**

My interpretation ~ The angels are acknowledging your emerging self. Keep going for you are growing. You are not the same person today that you were yesterday nor will you be the same person tomorrow that you are today.

Note: If today's message does not resonate with you, please practice discernment and choose not to accept it for yourself. I encourage you to go within to interpret the meaning of the messages for you specifically.

~ Day 21 to a New YOU! ~
Decision Making

It's not hard to make decisions
when you know what your values are.
~ Roy Disney

Making decisions is part of our daily life. Decisions may involve choosing what to eat as a meal or what to do for the day. These choices are relatively easy to make and don't require much thought or effort. On the other hand, each individual also has what I refer to as "bigger life decisions" to make. These choices may involve moving to a new location, starting or ending a career or business, starting or ending a relationship, starting or adding to the family and the list could go on and on.

I know that each individual has been faced with a multitude of decisions— some have been easier to make than others. The important thing to realize is that you have free will to make decisions, and that it is perfectly okay to choose again. Living life is all about having experiences. If we don't like the choice we made, we CAN choose again. I believe that many individuals have been conditioned to believe that once a choice has been made; you must live with your decision. From my perspective, that is the "old" way of thinking. I invite you to allow yourself the opportunity to choose again. It's okay to do so.

Of course you can ask others for their advice, but ultimately the decision is yours to make. No one else should have the power to make decisions for you. Remember, this is your life to live!

Please note that I am only referring to choices that you must make for yourself. Many times, there is another individual or individuals involved in situations and these situations require a consensus. It is imperative to discuss your feelings with all parties involved so that you feel good about the decision(s) you have made or are in the process of making. Compromising is necessary in some instances, but not at the expense of your health and well-being. Discuss the available options and ensure that the decision you make is one that you are happy with.

When considering that life is a journey and "pit stops" are necessary, it's important to recognize that it's okay to stop and ask directions when we need to. Road construction and detours may inhibit our path when we least expect it. Therefore, it is wise to check our map to ensure that we are headed in the right direction in order to reach our destination.

Questions to Consider

1. Do you find it easy / difficult to make decisions on your own without seeking the advice of others?

2. How do you feel about making decisions on your own?

3. How do you feel when you take the advice of others, which influences your decisions?

4. Have you had instances when you have compromised?

5. How do you feel when you have compromised?

Message to Uplift

Message for today ~ **Balance**

My interpretation ~ The angels are reminding you to have balance. Take time for you as you take time for others. Balance work with play. It is essential to have balance in your life.

Note: If today's message does not resonate with you, please practice discernment and choose not to accept it for yourself. I encourage you to go within to interpret the meaning of the messages for you specifically.

~ Day 22 to a New YOU! ~
Communicating Clearly

The most important thing in communication
is to hear what isn't being said.
*~ **Peter F. Drucker***

Present day communication surpasses just face-to-face contact. We can Skype, chat, talk on the phone, e-mail and text. The advances we have made in technology are nothing short of extraordinary. Effective communication involves communicating clearly, whether you are the sender or the receiver of the message.

Clearly speaking or conveying the message via written means is only part of communicating clearly. The other part involves being clear about what you are expressing. Be sure and say what you really mean thus avoiding any doubt for the listener or reader. Be clear when expressing what you mean. Sometimes, you have to spell-it-out rather than being vague. Having to "read between the lines" inhibits effective communication – both for the sender and the receiver.

We have two ears and one mouth
so that we can listen twice as much as we speak.
~ Epictetus

Remember, communication involves both listening and speaking. Pay attention to the verbal and nonverbal feedback you are receiving during communication whether it is in-person, over the phone or via written word. Being an effective listener may require you to relay back to the sender what you have heard and interpreted in order to make sure that you have heard the message correctly.

Questions to Consider

1. How would you assess your communication skills?

2. Do you communicate clearly?

3. Do you listen effectively?

Message to Uplift

Message for today ~ **Enchantment**

My interpretation ~ The angels are acknowledging enchantment. The feeling of peace, joy, love, bliss and happiness is within you and surrounds you. Embrace this feeling of enchantment freely and fully.

Note: If today's message does not resonate with you, please practice discernment and choose not to accept it for yourself. I encourage you to go within to interpret the meaning of the messages for you specifically.

~ Day 23 to a New YOU! ~
Non-Attachment to the Outcome

I know what I have given you.
I do not know what you have received.
~ Antonio Porchia

Remember that each individual will have their own perception of an experience. It is next to impossible to alter someone's perception. As I have mentioned previously, in circumstances that you don't see "eye-to-eye," simply listen and then practice non-attachment to the outcome. This means that you are recognizing what you have heard, but you are not allowing another individual's perception to influence your own.

Another example would be when someone asks for your advice or opinion, and they don't like what you have said. Acknowledge the variance of opinions, and then release it. There is no need to feed it any energy or wonder if you should have said it differently. Both of you are having your own human life experience, which involves your own perception and freewill. Speaking your truth with love and conviction is necessary. Do not be afraid to do so simply because you are not sure how the message will be received.

As the receiver of a message, I encourage you to not take things personally as well. The sender of the message may mean one thing and you perceive it to be something else. Go through the entire range of emotions you are feeling. Now, step back and observe. Ask yourself, why do I feel this way? What part of me is causing me to react in this manner? Then, choose to observe the message differently or even ask the sender exactly what they meant.

Questions to Consider

1. When asked for advice or my opinion by others, I tend to _____.

2. In doing so, I feel _____.

3. When communicating with others, I tend to _____.

4. In doing so, I feel _____.

5. How do you feel when a phone call is not returned or an email is not responded to?

Message to Uplift

Message for today ~ **Intention**

My interpretation ~ The angels are acknowledging intention. Be mindful of why you do what you do. Is your intention coming from a place of love or from fear?

Note: If today's message does not resonate with you, please practice discernment and choose not to accept it for yourself. I encourage you to go within to interpret the meaning of the messages for you specifically.

~ Day 24 to a New YOU! ~
Having Patience with the Process

Patience and perseverance have a magical effect
before which difficulties disappear
and obstacles vanish.
*~ **John Quincy Adams***

Have patience with the process. Change takes time. Rest when you need to. Do not get upset if you feel like you are not making progress because you ARE! Some days, you may feel like you are taking a step backwards or you may feel like you are having a self-perceived "bad" day. Honor yourself and what you are feeling. This is part of the process of transformation. Patience truly is a virtue!

Growth takes time. Remember, a seed doesn't become a flower overnight! It takes soil, water, nurturing (pulling the surrounding weeds), and sunlight, which translates spiritually to taking time for you as well as basking in the love and light! We can observe the change that is occurring, but the flower doesn't grow any faster.

It is also vitally important to remember that we are a continual work-in-progress, and there is always room for improvement. Each day is a new beginning; therefore, we will each have new life experiences with each day new. New experiences sometimes involve challenges. It's up to you if you choose to view the challenge as the proverbial mountain or mole-hill.

Questions to Consider

1. How would you rate your patience level?

2. How would you rate your patience level when assessing the progress you are making with your transformation?

3. Do you recognize the progress you are making?

4. Do you recognize the progress you have made?

5. What areas do you feel still need to be addressed as you continue to progress?

Message to Uplift

Message for today ~ **Trust**

My interpretation ~ The angels are reminding you to trust. Trust that all is as it should be in this moment and in every moment. Trust in the process. Trust that all is well.

Note: If today's message does not resonate with you, please practice discernment and choose not to accept it for yourself. I encourage you to go within to interpret the meaning of the messages for you specifically.

~ Day 25 to a New YOU! ~
Shining Your Light Bright

Our deepest fear is not that we are inadequate.
Our deepest fear is that we are powerful beyond measure.
It is our light, not our darkness that most frightens us.
We ask ourselves, who am I to be brilliant,
gorgeous, talented and fabulous?

Actually, who are you not to be?
You are a child of God.
Your playing small doesn't serve the world.

There's nothing enlightened about shrinking
so that other people won't feel insecure around you.
We were born to manifest the glory of God that is within us.
It's not just in some of us; it is in everyone.

As we let our own light shine,
we unconsciously give other people
permission to do the same.
As we are liberated from our own fear
our presence automatically liberates others.
*~ **Marianne Williamson***

This quote by Marianne Williamson had an enormous impact on my life the first time I read it. Actually, every time I read it, I have that same feeling of empowerment wash over me. It is the perfect reminder for me to shine my own light bright, and I encourage you to do the same.

The time is now for you to shine your light bright! Each one of us has the Divine spark within us. It is our right to be all that we are intended to be and so much more. Do not allow anyone to dim your light under any circumstances. This is your life, you are creating it, and you have the power to choose. You are perfect and whole in every way. Shine your light brightly! As the song lyrics emphasize, *This little Light of mine, I'm gonna let it shine...let it shine, let it shine, let it shine...*

Let your Light shine bright!

Honoring your Light Exercise

Silence your mind chatter and sit in quiet contemplation. Take a moment to perceive what your Light is and what shining your Light truly means to you. Spend time in reflection and appreciate the magnificent capacity you behold within you. Allow memories to gently surface into your conscious mind of when your Light had been dimmed by others as well as when you dimmed your Light yourself by choice. Allow powerful memories to fill your body, mind and soul of when you shined your Light bright. Take note of any feelings you experience as you do so.

Questions to Consider

1. Recalling instances when my light has been dimmed, I felt _____.

2. Recalling instances when my light has been allowed to shine, I felt _____.

Affirmation to Assist You

Affirm ~ I honor the Light within me. I honor the Light within me. I honor the Light within me.

Message to Uplift

Message for today ~ **Truth & Integrity**

My interpretation ~ The angels are acknowledging truth and integrity. Align your thoughts, words, and actions with your beliefs. Walk your talk and talk your walk.

Note: If today's message does not resonate with you, please practice discernment and choose not to accept it for yourself. I encourage you to go within to interpret the meaning of the messages for you specifically.

~ Day 26 to a New YOU! ~
Living Authentically

A good character is the best tombstone.
Those who loved you and were helped by you
will remember you
when forget-me-nots have withered.
Carve your name on hearts, not on marble.
~ Charles H. Spurgeon

I believe that living authentically involves being genuine with all people you come into contact with. This means not being afraid to be yourself or to feel the need to hide certain aspects of yourself due to fear of what others may think. It's necessary to allow the "real deal" to shine through always. In other words, you are aligning your thoughts, words, and actions with your beliefs. You are walking your talk and talking your walk.

In addition, I feel that it is necessary to always be conscious of the energy you are putting out into the

Universe. Being mindful of the words you choose to express is being considerate of others' feelings yet still being authentic. It's important to honor and respect everyone's beliefs yet not always energetically appropriate to share your own in my opinion. In no way do I feel that if you choose to remain silent are you being less than authentic. Rather, I feel that you are simply being compassionate. There is a difference.

The time is now to start living your life the way you want to be remembered. Focus your energy on being the best you can be and living a life without regret so that you can live fully.

Questions to Consider

1. Are you living an authentic life?

2. Are your thoughts, words, and actions in alignment?

3. Are you the same person around everyone?

Message to Uplift

Message for today ~ **Dreams**

My interpretation ~ The angels are acknowledging your dreams. No dream is too big to achieve nor too small to undertake. Dream big and dream often!

Note: If today's message does not resonate with you, please practice discernment and choose not to accept it for yourself. I encourage you to go within to interpret the meaning of the messages for you specifically.

~ Day 27 to a New YOU! ~
Taking Time For You

It is only when we silent the blaring sounds
of our daily existence
that we can finally hear the whispers of truth
that life reveals to us,
as it stands knocking on the doorsteps of our hearts.
~ K.T. Jong

Without a doubt, I'm sure you have no problem doing what others want or need you to do. Sure, there might be something else that you prefer to be doing. You may even feel a bit frustrated when performing the task or attending the event. Nonetheless, you are still taking time for others and their needs.

Let's approach this day with a different thought— take time for YOU today. Give to yourself! You are worthy and you deserve it. Simply taking time doesn't have a monetary cost, yet it creates abundance in the form of happiness and health.

Individuals should have balance in their life. Having balance involves taking time for others and taking time for oneself. You may feel "stretched thin" if you do not have this balance. Notice how I have used the word "take" rather than "make." There are 24 hours in a day. A new day begins when those hours are expended. We are unable to make the day longer; therefore, we cannot make time. We can only take time.

For clarification purposes, having balance does not mean that you have to be critical of the time factor and devote an equal amount of time to each in order to have balance. Rather, the intention of having balance is what matters.

Questions to Consider

1. If factors such as time and money do not play a role, what would you do today?

2. What would you do every day?

3. Review the answers that you have written. How do you feel when you read then?

4. If factors such as time and money do play a role, what would you do today?

5. What would you do every day?

6. Review the answers that you have written. How do you feel when you read then?

Message to Uplift

Message for today ~ **Friendship**

My interpretation ~ The angels are acknowledging the importance of friendship. Choose to tell those people in your life what they really mean to you. Leave no words unspoken today and every day.

Note: If today's message does not resonate with you, please practice discernment and choose not to accept it for yourself. I encourage you to go within to interpret the meaning of the messages for you specifically.

~ Day 28 to a New YOU! ~
Celebrating You

Find what makes your heart sing
and create your own music.
~ Mac Anderson

Your Birthday is your special day! Your Birthday is the day in which your family and friends celebrate you and your entry into the Earth plane. Why limit this celebration to one day? Celebrate YOU and all that you are each and every day.

Rejoice in All That Is! I see that you are an AMAZING individual. See yourself as an AMAZING individual as well. Say aloud and say it proud, "I AM AMAZING!"

Allow yourself to really feel how amazing you are. Celebrate all that you are and all that you are becoming.

You are making a difference in the lives of others by simply being YOU. No extra work is required. By setting an example and shining your Light bright, you allow others to do the same. Do not doubt the power that you hold within.

Celebrate YOU!

You are AMAZING!

Questions to Consider

1. When it's my Birthday, I feel _____.

2. I find it easy / difficult to celebrate me.

3. When celebrating me, I feel _____.

4. I recognize that I am _____.

Message to Uplift

Message for today ~ **Guardian Angel**

My interpretation ~ The angels are acknowledging your guardian angel. You are safe, secure, protected and loved beyond measure. You are not alone.

Note: If today's message does not resonate with you, please practice discernment and choose not to accept it for yourself. I encourage you to go within to interpret the meaning of the messages for you specifically.

~ Conclusion ~

Although this book has ended, I encourage you to continue to implement the suggestions as you are guided to do so. Just as my journey continues, so does yours. My hope is that you have grown from what I have shared with you and that the insight and tools I have provided for you will continue to facilitate you on your spiritual journey. In addition, I encourage you to share your journey with others because we are all teachers just as we are students.

My motivation in life is to be happy and to live life fully without regret. As I have stated before, there are two ways to view everything— through the eyes of love and through the eyes of fear. I choose to view life through the eyes of love and to assist others in doing the same. Day one to a new you began with loving you. I encourage you to continue to love yourself and believe that anything is possible. Remember this is your time! I encourage you to live an authentic life, be the best you can be, and love yourself in the process.

Much love and many blessings to YOU!

Shelly

*Open your heart to love
and to be loved.*

~ About Shelly ~

Intuitive Medium, Reiki Master and Spiritual Teacher Shelly Wilson would love to assist you on your spiritual journey. With respect, truth, integrity and love, Shelly honors your free will and recognizes that you are co-creating your reality with the Universe. She offers private readings, intuitive coaching, Reiki sessions, and teaches workshops. *The Shelly Wilson Show* airs live each Wednesday at 2:00 pm CST on Blog Talk Radio.

www.ShellyRWilson.com

www.Facebook.com/IntuitiveMediumShelly

www.BlogTalkRadio.com/ShellyWilson